What Rots?

Sarah Fleming

Contents

OXFORD
UNIVERSITY PRESS

What is rot?

Rot makes things go soft or bad.

Rot breaks things down. It needs:
- time
- air
- water
- heat.

100 days

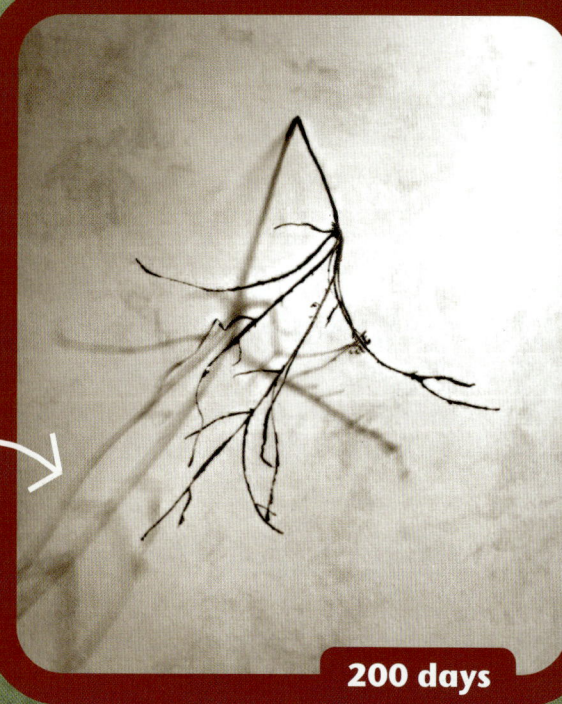

200 days

Some things rot fast.

This wood has been here for ten years.

Bacteria and fungus help things to rot.

Some things rot slowly.

Plant rot

Old food and plants rot. They make food for new plants.

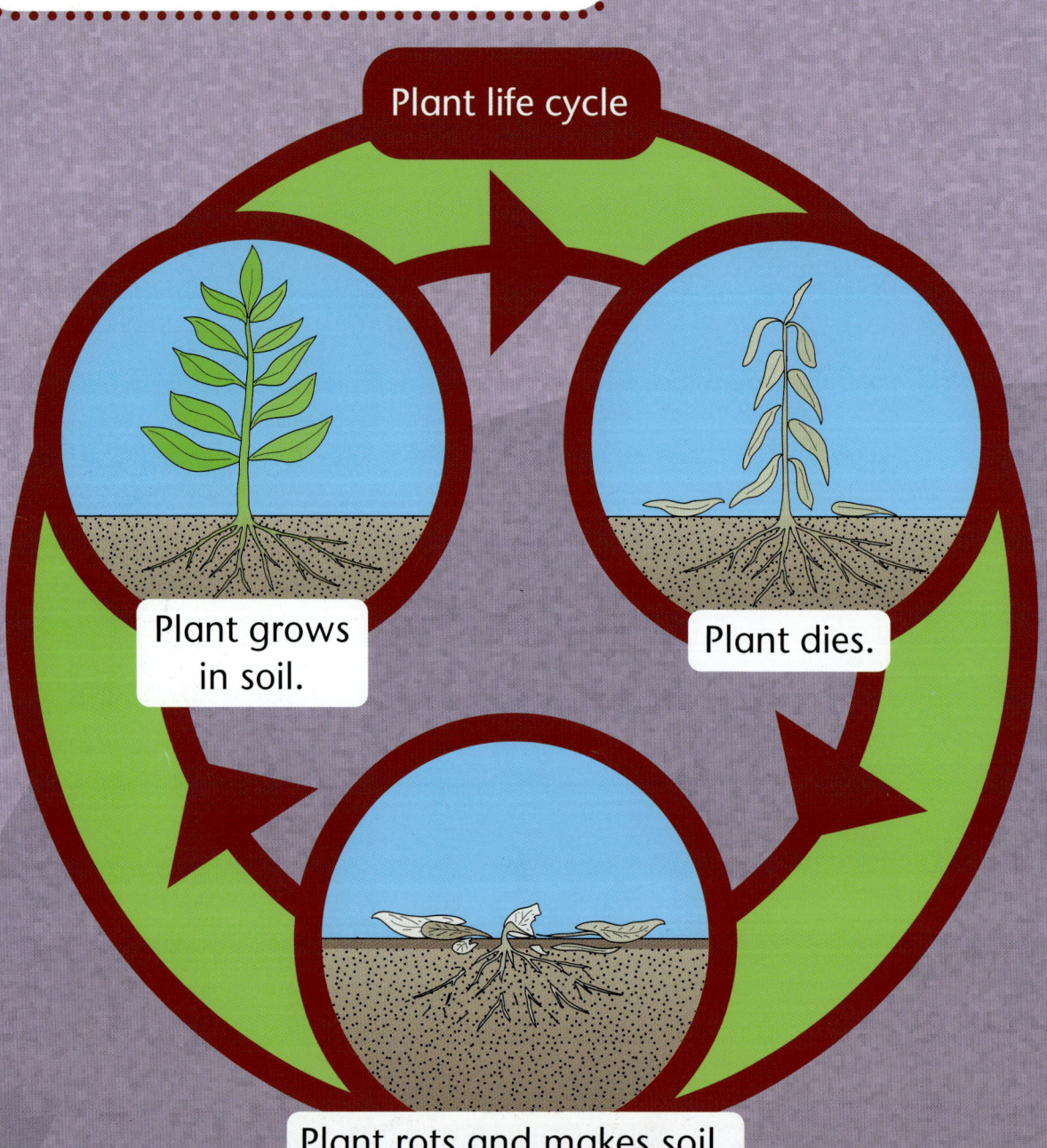

Plant life cycle

Plant grows in soil.

Plant dies.

Plant rots and makes soil.

Compost is made from old plants and food.

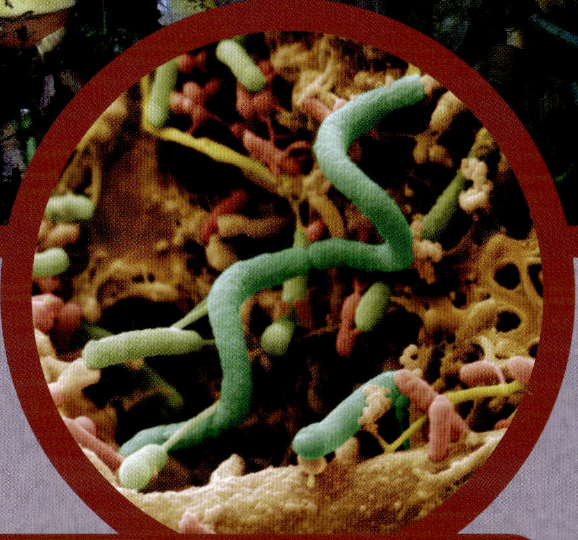

Bacteria make the compost rot.

This fork is rotting.

Some plastic is now made from plants so it can rot, like this fork.

Animal rot

Animals rot. They make food for new plants and animals.

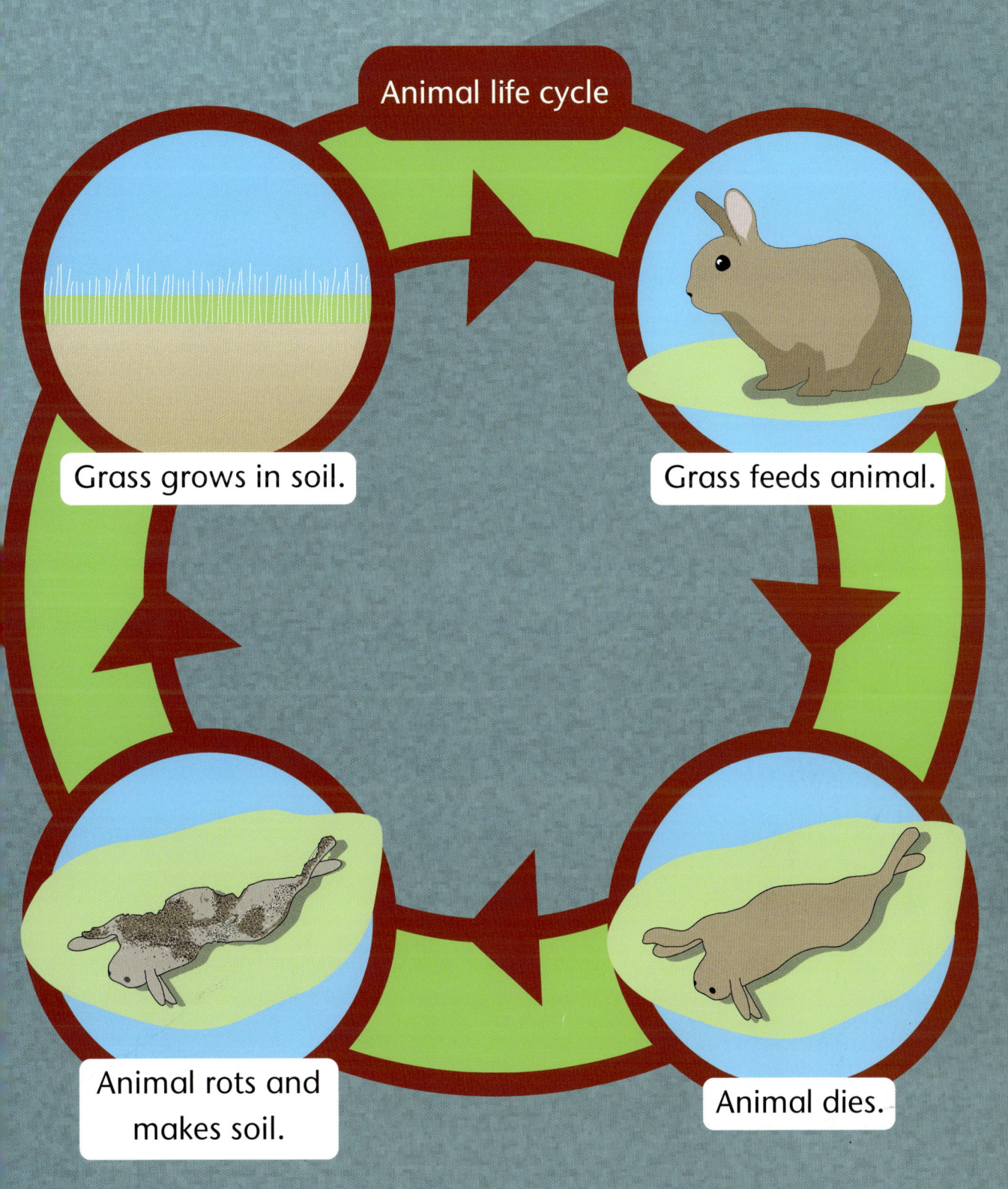

Animal life cycle

Grass grows in soil.

Grass feeds animal.

Animal rots and makes soil.

Animal dies.

7

Wood rot

Dry rot eats wood.

Wet rot eats wood.

Body rot

People can rot.

1855, Crimean War Hospital

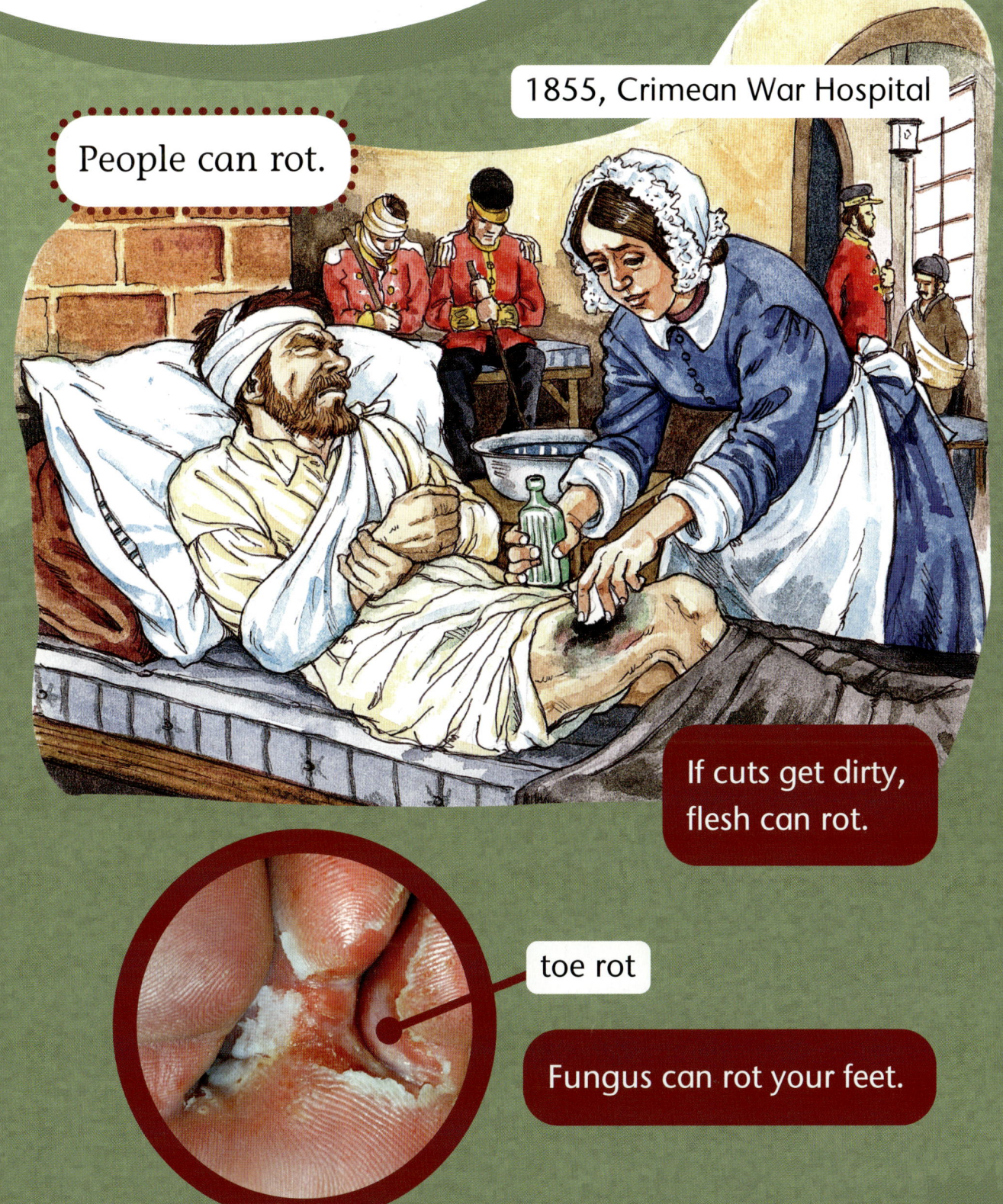

If cuts get dirty, flesh can rot.

toe rot

Fungus can rot your feet.

Tooth rot

Sweets and fizzy drinks rot teeth.

Tiny microbes eat the sweet things on teeth. They also eat teeth and gums.

Do this test. You need:

2 teeth

fizzy sweet drink

tap water

2 glasses

1. Put the drinks in the glasses.
2. Add the teeth.
3. Look at the teeth every day for a week.

tap water

fizzy sweet drink

Day 2

Day 7

Food rot

These foods are rotting. What are they?

A

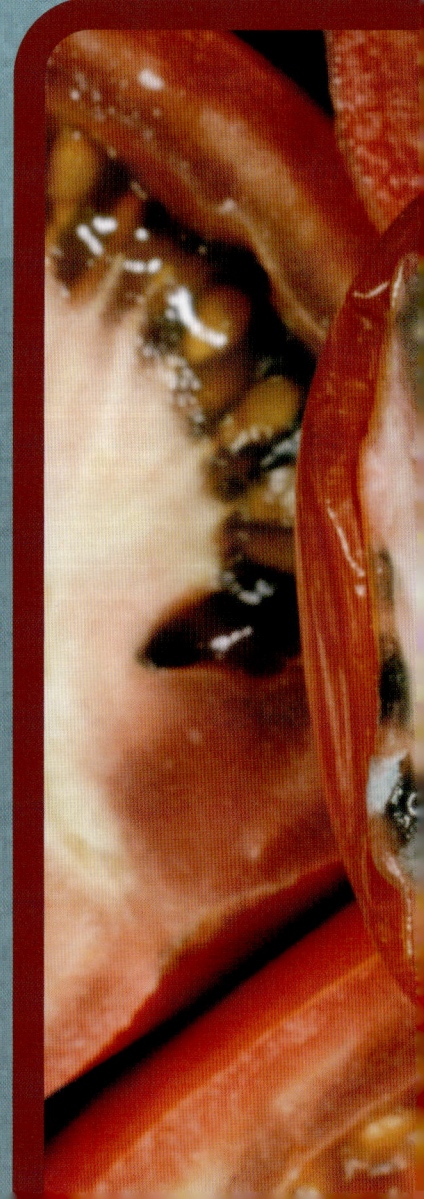

B

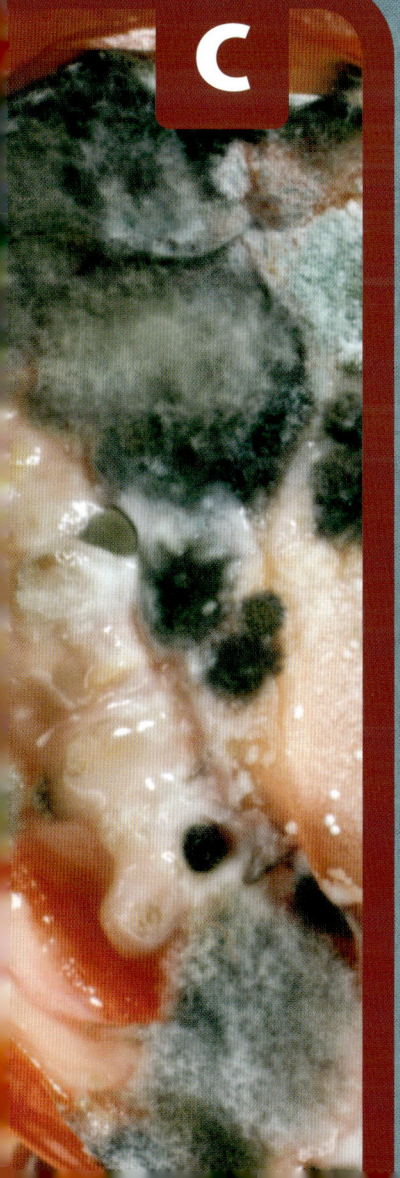

C

D

This rotting food can be made into very sweet wine.

13

Stop the rot

We can't stop rot. But we can slow it down.

Keep things cold.

Dry things out.

Cover with chemicals.

Make bodies into mummies.

Good or bad?

Is rot good or bad?

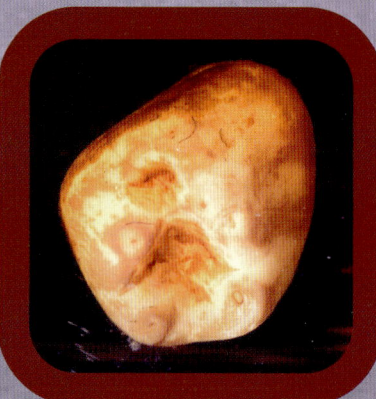
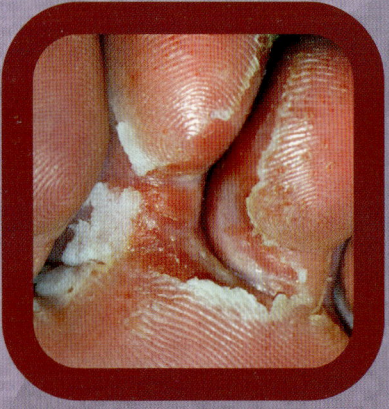

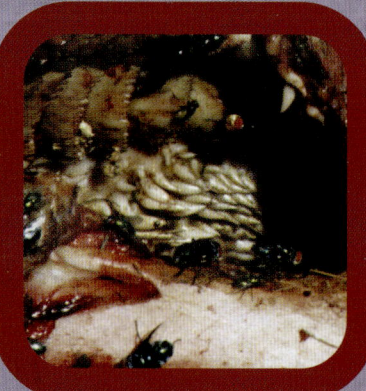